DIAL-AN-ANIMAL

INSTANT GUIDE TO GIANT SEA CREATURES

Written by Gina Phillips
Illustrated by F.S. Persico

kidsbooks Incorporated

Copyright © 1989 Kidsbooks, Inc.
7004 N. California Ave.
Chicago, Il. 60645

ISBN: #0-942025-69-5
All Rights reserved including the right
of reproduction in whole or in part in any form.

Manufactured in the United States of America

Marlins and sailfish are known as billfish because of their long, pointed upper jaws. Billfish attack groups of smaller fish using their sword-shaped bills like clubs. In this manner, billfish can stun and kill a large number of prey at a time. Billfish are among the fastest swimmers in the sea.

Marlins are found in warm waters throughout the world. The biggest marlin, called the black marlin, lives in the Pacific Ocean. Black marlins can weigh more than 1,000 pounds. Marlins have incredible power. They have been known to accidentally drive their bills through 13 inches of solid wood!

The sailfish gets its name from the dorsal fin on its back. When opened, this fin is so huge that it looks like a sail. Usually measuring seven or eight feet in length, sailfish can weigh up to 300 pounds. A sailfish has been timed at 60 miles per hour, making it the fastest swimmer of all sea creatures. Sailfish live in the tropical waters of the Atlantic Ocean and the Caribbean Sea.

The ocean sunfish can be found in all tropical waters. Shaped like a giant disk, this fish can measure 12 feet from top to bottom and weigh 3,000 pounds. The ocean sunfish has almost no tail fin. Large upper and lower fins balance it as it glides slowly through the water, sometimes swimming near the surface.

The tough, leathery skin of the ocean sunfish has no scales. Instead, its skin is coated with a slimy film and covered with prickles. Its small mouth is full of teeth. This creature feeds on jellyfish and can even eat the poisonous Portuguese man-of-war without being harmed.

The ocean sunfish lays more eggs than any other animal, 300 million at a time.

Blown along by the wind, the Portuguese man-of-war drifts on the surface of the water. Dangling beneath a gas-filled sack, called a float, are poisonous tentacles that measure up to 75 feet long. The deadly tentacles kill fish on which the man-of-war feeds. This giant creature can produce very painful stings if touched by a human.

The Portuguese man-of-war is found in the warmer parts of oceans throughout the world.

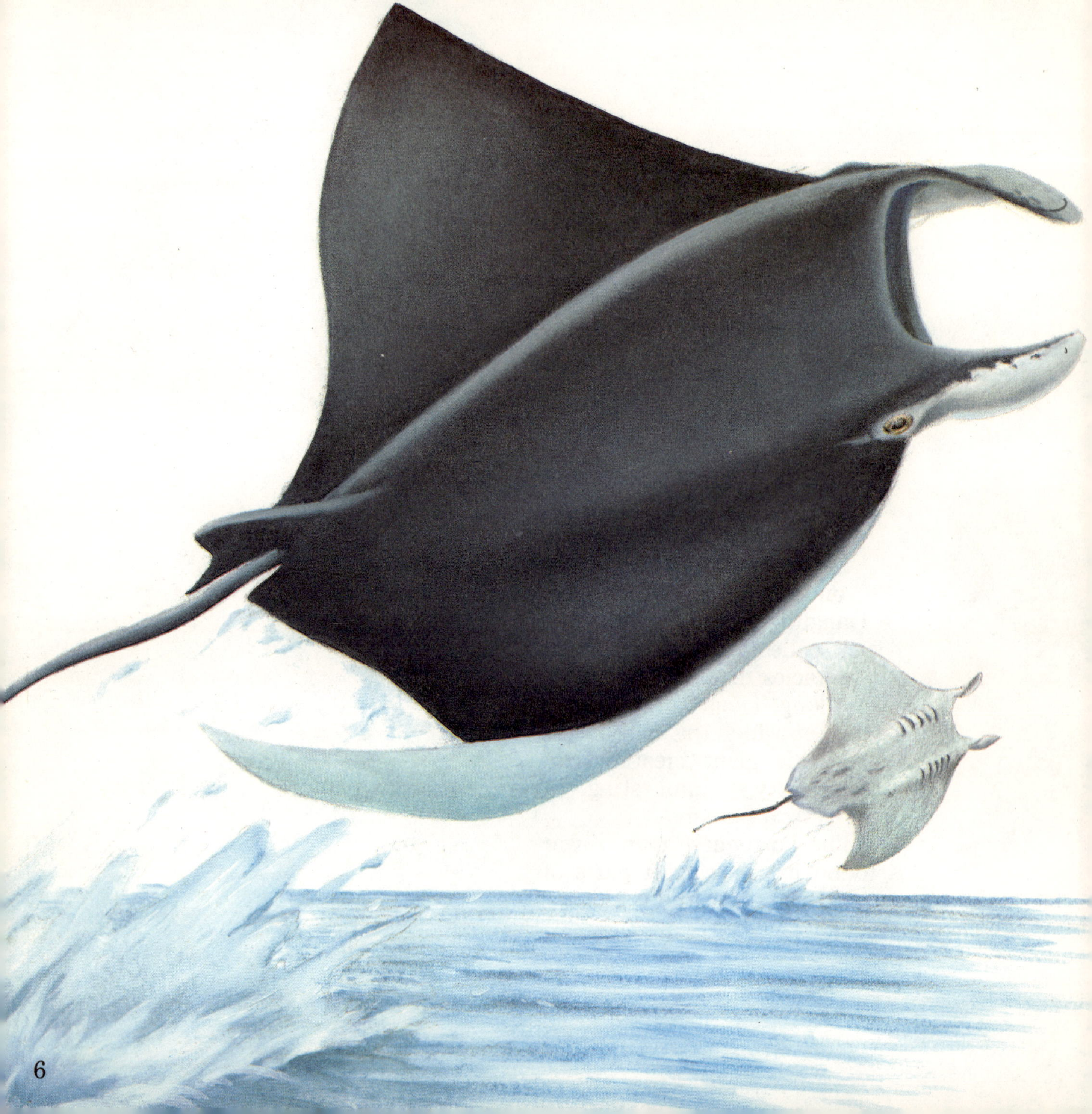

The manta ray is the largest of more than 300 species of rays and skates. Measuring as much as 22 feet across and weighing up to 3,000 pounds, the manta ray swims through the water by flapping its huge "wings." Most rays prefer to stay hidden under a layer of sand on the ocean floor, but the manta swims and feeds near the water's surface.

Related to the shark, mantas are found in both the Atlantic and Pacific oceans. Among sharklike fish, the manta's brain is the largest. This harmless giant uses the flaps on either side of its head to direct tiny animals into its huge mouth.

On rare occasions, manta rays have been seen leaping out of the water and even giving birth to their young while in midair!

The dangerous barracuda is often called the "tiger of the sea." Long, lean, and swift, this fierce fish has many sharp teeth in its lengthy jaws. When hunting, the barracuda stays very still and waits until a school of fish swims close. Then it darts forward and zeros in on a single fish, ignoring all the others. Sometimes barracudas swim and hunt in groups.

Barracudas will attack almost anything, including humans. Although some species grow to 6 feet, most are smaller. One bite from a barracuda can severely wound a swimmer's arm or leg. The barracuda, unlike the shark, leaves a clean wound and makes only a single attack.

Barracudas are mainly found in the warm waters near Florida and the West Indies.

Even though whales look like fish, they are not. Whales, like humans, are mammals. Whales breathe air, are warm-blooded, give birth to live babies, and feed those babies with milk from their bodies.

Whales are divided into two groups, baleen whales and toothed whales. Baleen whales have no teeth. Instead, they have comblike filters called baleen attached to their upper jaws. Their baleen is used to strain tiny plants and animals—called plankton—out of the water. Toothed whales hunt and use their sharp teeth to seize their prey.

The largest animal that has ever lived—larger even than any known dinosaur—is the blue whale. The blue whale can reach a length of 110 feet and weigh 300,000 pounds (more than 20 elephants!). This giant sea creature survives by eating plankton. A blue whale can eat 9,000 pounds of plankton each day.

Blue whales make a variety of noises and calls. These noises can be heard by other whales miles away. Females have a single baby, called a calf, which grows at the incredible rate of almost ten pounds every hour. In two years, the calf can grow to 75 feet long and weigh 250,000 pounds. Blue whales may live 80 years or more and are found in all oceans of the world.

The 65-foot bowhead whale lives in the icy waters of the Arctic Ocean. A two-foot-thick layer of blubber helps keep it warm.

Bowhead Whale

Bowheads swim near the water's surface with their mouths open. Floating plankton is sifted through their 12-foot-long baleen. The bowhead uses its 8,000-pound tongue to push the sea water back out through its baleen filters which catch the plankton.

The bowhead whale is on the endangered species list.

Blue Whale

11

The fin whale is a baleen whale and is the second-largest sea creature. It can grow to a length of more than 70 feet and weigh 150,000 pounds.

Killer whales belong to the toothed whale group. They are excellent hunters and often work together to catch prey. Mostly they hunt seals, penguins, and fish. Weighing 16,000 pounds, killer whales are very strong and can leap 20 feet into the air. These intelligent animals are famous for their ability to learn tricks and perform in water shows.

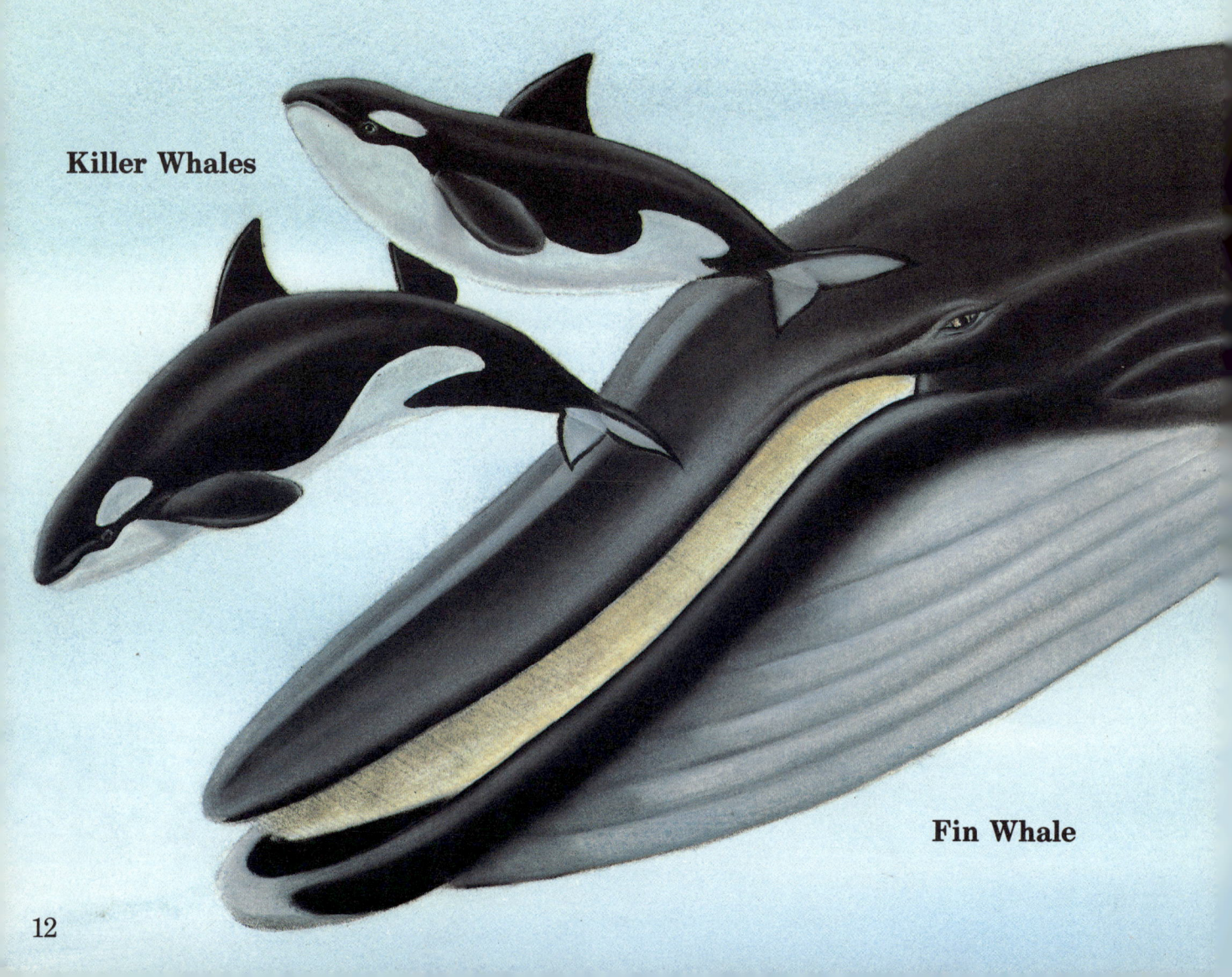

Killer Whales

Fin Whale

Another baleen whale is the humpback. This whale is easily identified by the long, knobby flippers that run nearly one third the length of its body. Humpbacks get their name from the way they curve their backs above the surface of the water just before they dive. These 50-foot-long giants can sometimes be seen close to land. Many recordings have been made of the humpback's unusual "singing," which can last for 20 minutes at a time.

Humpback Whale

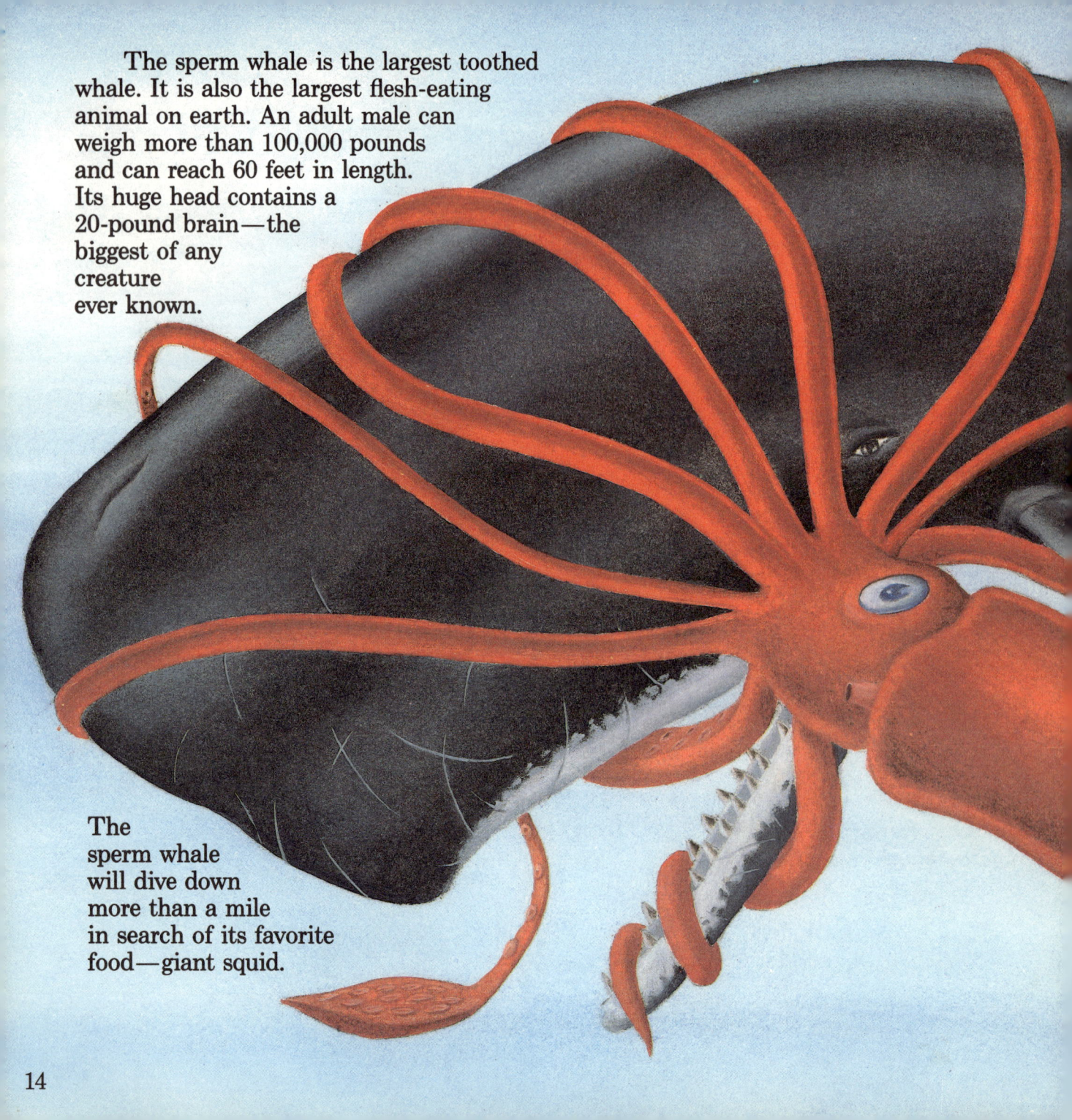

The sperm whale is the largest toothed whale. It is also the largest flesh-eating animal on earth. An adult male can weigh more than 100,000 pounds and can reach 60 feet in length. Its huge head contains a 20-pound brain—the biggest of any creature ever known.

The sperm whale will dive down more than a mile in search of its favorite food—giant squid.

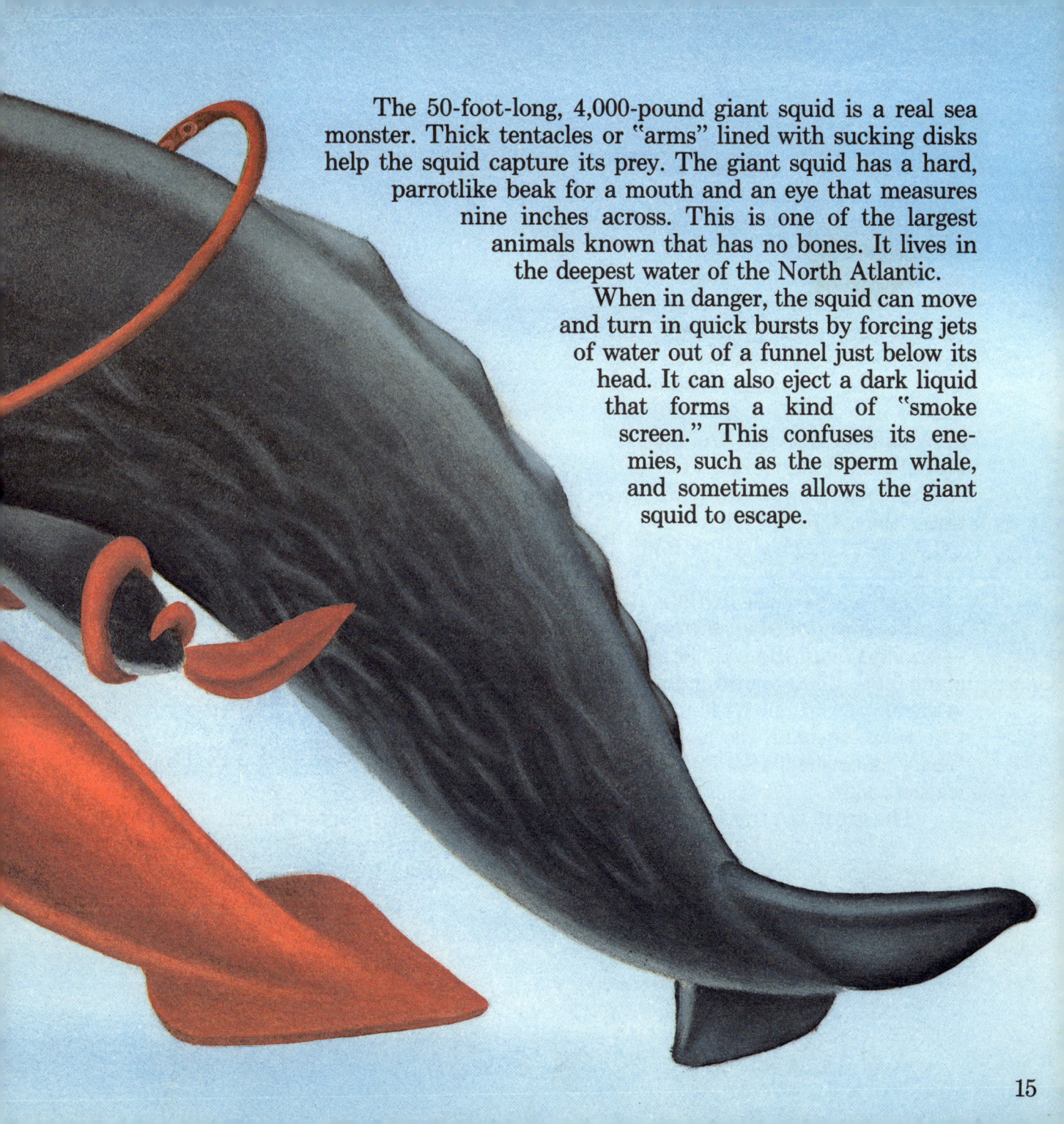

The 50-foot-long, 4,000-pound giant squid is a real sea monster. Thick tentacles or "arms" lined with sucking disks help the squid capture its prey. The giant squid has a hard, parrotlike beak for a mouth and an eye that measures nine inches across. This is one of the largest animals known that has no bones. It lives in the deepest water of the North Atlantic.

When in danger, the squid can move and turn in quick bursts by forcing jets of water out of a funnel just below its head. It can also eject a dark liquid that forms a kind of "smoke screen." This confuses its enemies, such as the sperm whale, and sometimes allows the giant squid to escape.

Most sea turtles are found in warm oceans throughout the world. The enormous front flippers of giant sea turtles enable them to move rapidly through the water. Despite their great size, they are very graceful swimmers. The females come ashore only to lay eggs—150 at a time. The eggs are the size of Ping-Pong balls. They remain covered in a sandy pit until they hatch. Then the baby turtles quickly set off for the sea.

The leatherback turtle is by far the largest of all turtles —on land or in the sea. This eight-foot, 1,500-pound giant is the only sea turtle without a true shell. Instead, the leatherback is covered with tough, leathery skin.

The green sea turtle gets its name from the greenish color of its fat. This reptile has long been prized by humans as a valuable food source. The 600-pound green sea turtle sleeps floating on its back on the water's surface.

Leatherback Turtle

Green Sea Turtle

The moray eel lives in the rocks and coral reefs of tropical waters. With its sharp, pointed teeth, snakelike body and mouth shaped into a permanent grin, the moray eel looks frightening indeed.

Morays average five feet in length, but some giants have been found that are more than 10 feet long. Although moray eels are not known to attack humans, they will deliver a jagged, painful bite if disturbed.

The giant grouper has a huge mouth. It captures its meals by swallowing so strongly that any small fish nearby is sucked into its mouth! This giant warm-water fish grows up to 12 feet in length and weighs about 1,000 pounds.

The giant clam has a shell four feet wide and can weigh more than 500 pounds. These huge shellfish can trap a diver by clamping down on an arm or leg.

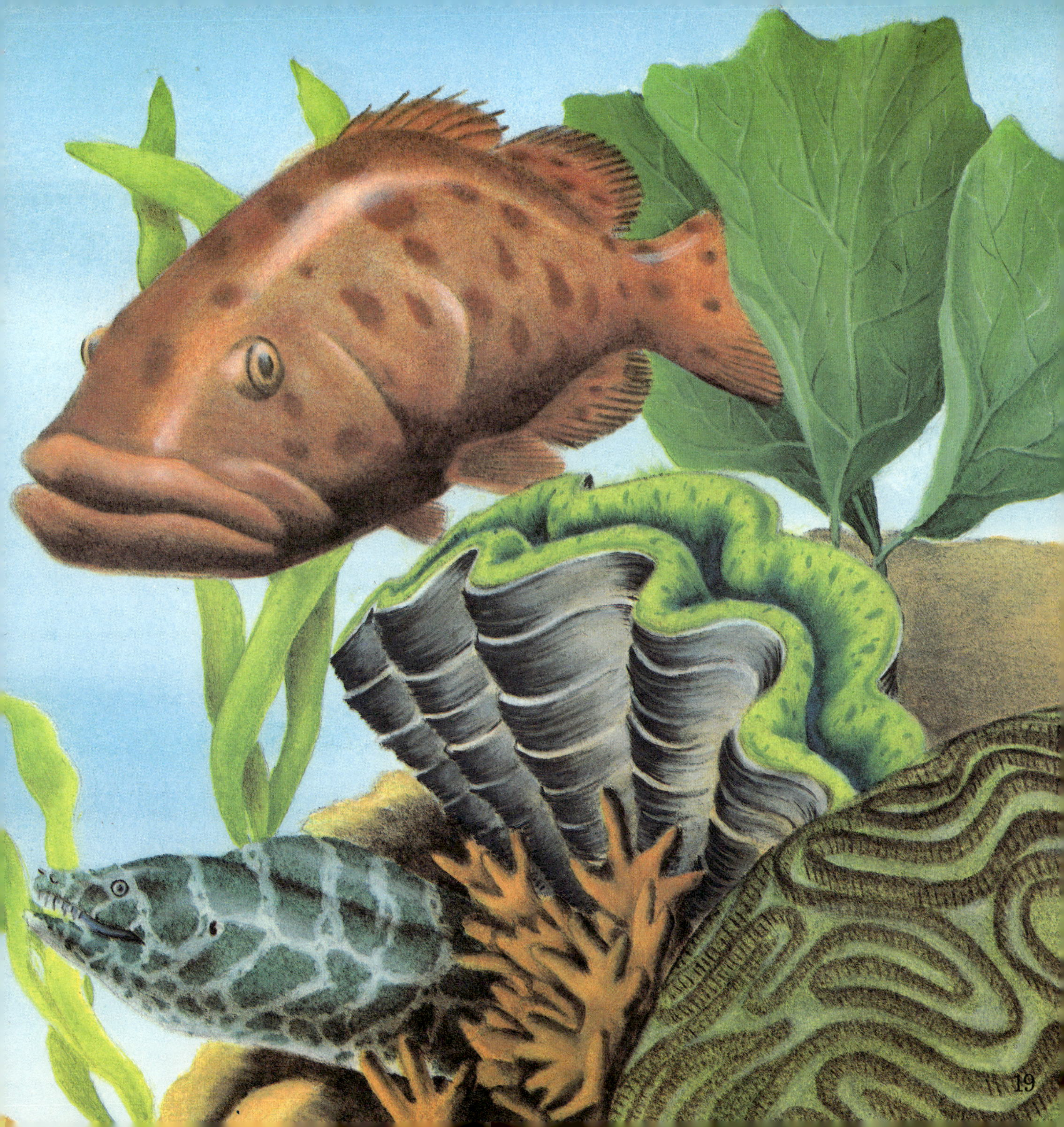

Sharks were swimming in the ocean 200 million years before dinosaurs even existed. In the millions of years since, sharks have hardly changed at all. Today, more than 300 kinds of sharks can be found in the seas of the world.

Sharks are different from most other fish. Most fish have a skeleton made of bone. Shark skeletons are made of a softer material called cartilage—the same material that forms the bridge of your nose. Most fish can stay still in the water. Sharks will sink the moment they stop swimming, so they must constantly keep moving. Instead of having slippery, smooth fish scales, a shark's skin is so rough it feels like sandpaper. All bony fish have one gill opening on each side to let water flow through. Sharks have five or more gills.

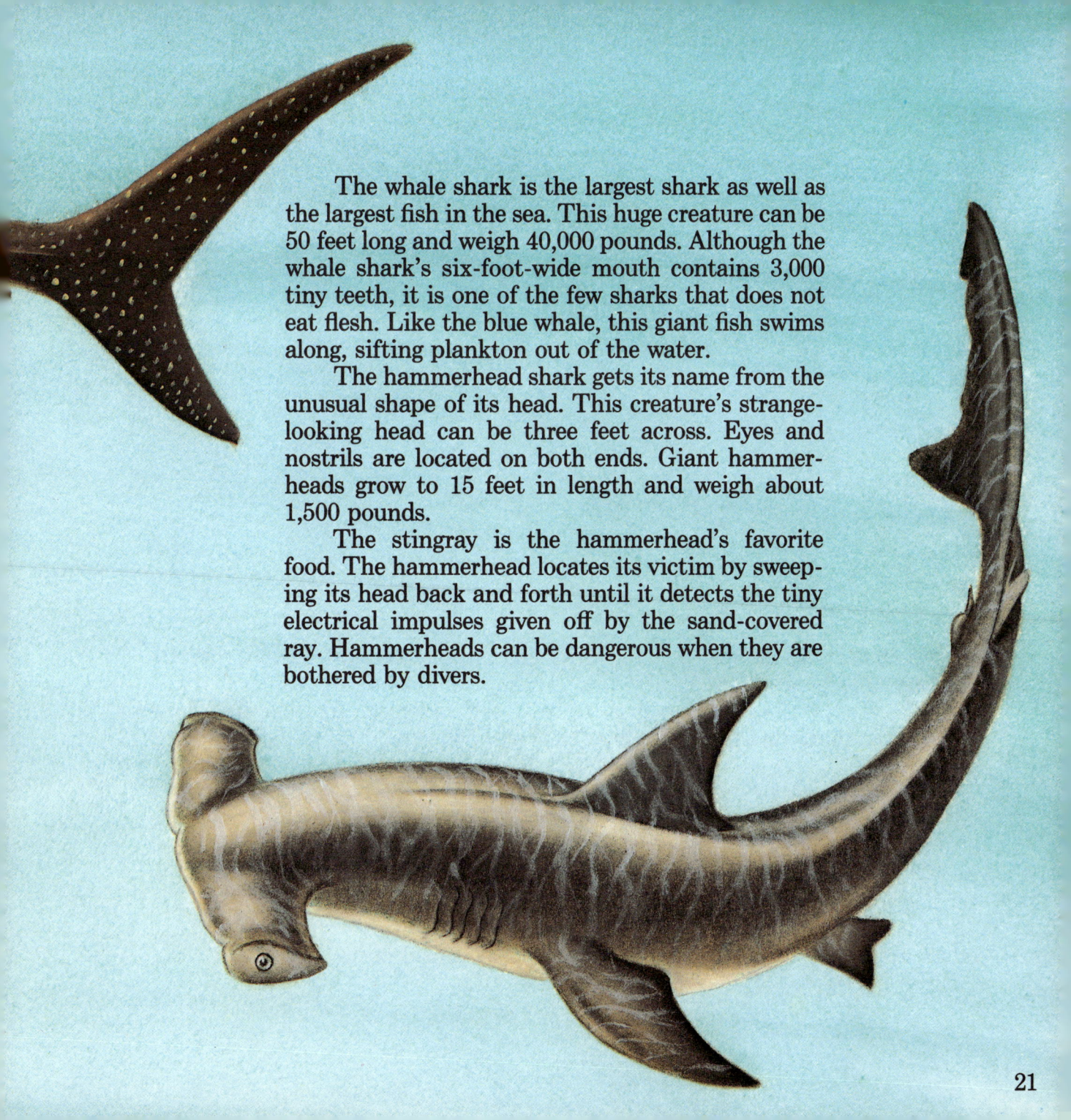

The whale shark is the largest shark as well as the largest fish in the sea. This huge creature can be 50 feet long and weigh 40,000 pounds. Although the whale shark's six-foot-wide mouth contains 3,000 tiny teeth, it is one of the few sharks that does not eat flesh. Like the blue whale, this giant fish swims along, sifting plankton out of the water.

The hammerhead shark gets its name from the unusual shape of its head. This creature's strange-looking head can be three feet across. Eyes and nostrils are located on both ends. Giant hammerheads grow to 15 feet in length and weigh about 1,500 pounds.

The stingray is the hammerhead's favorite food. The hammerhead locates its victim by sweeping its head back and forth until it detects the tiny electrical impulses given off by the sand-covered ray. Hammerheads can be dangerous when they are bothered by divers.

Of all flesh-eating sharks, great white sharks are the largest. In fact, they are the largest flesh-eating fish of any kind. These sea monsters will eat prey of any size. The great white shark can grow to be 20 feet in length. Its three-inch-long teeth are so sharp that the great white can cut a 500-pound fish in half with one bite!

Great whites are mainly surface feeders. They can sense the slightest vibration in the water caused by a wounded fish or a swimming human. They also have an excellent sense of smell. A great white can detect one part of blood in 100 million parts of water—and even know what direction the smell is coming from!

More attacks on humans have been made by the great white than by any other shark. Most sharks, however, are shy and fearful of humans.

Flesh-eating sharks have powerful jaws and teeth. Some of them can bite through thick steel plate. Lost teeth can be replaced by the shark again and again—sometimes within 24 hours!

When sharks feed in groups, they sometimes attack prey with great energy. Then they will bite anything, including other sharks and even themselves! Such behavior is called a feeding frenzy.

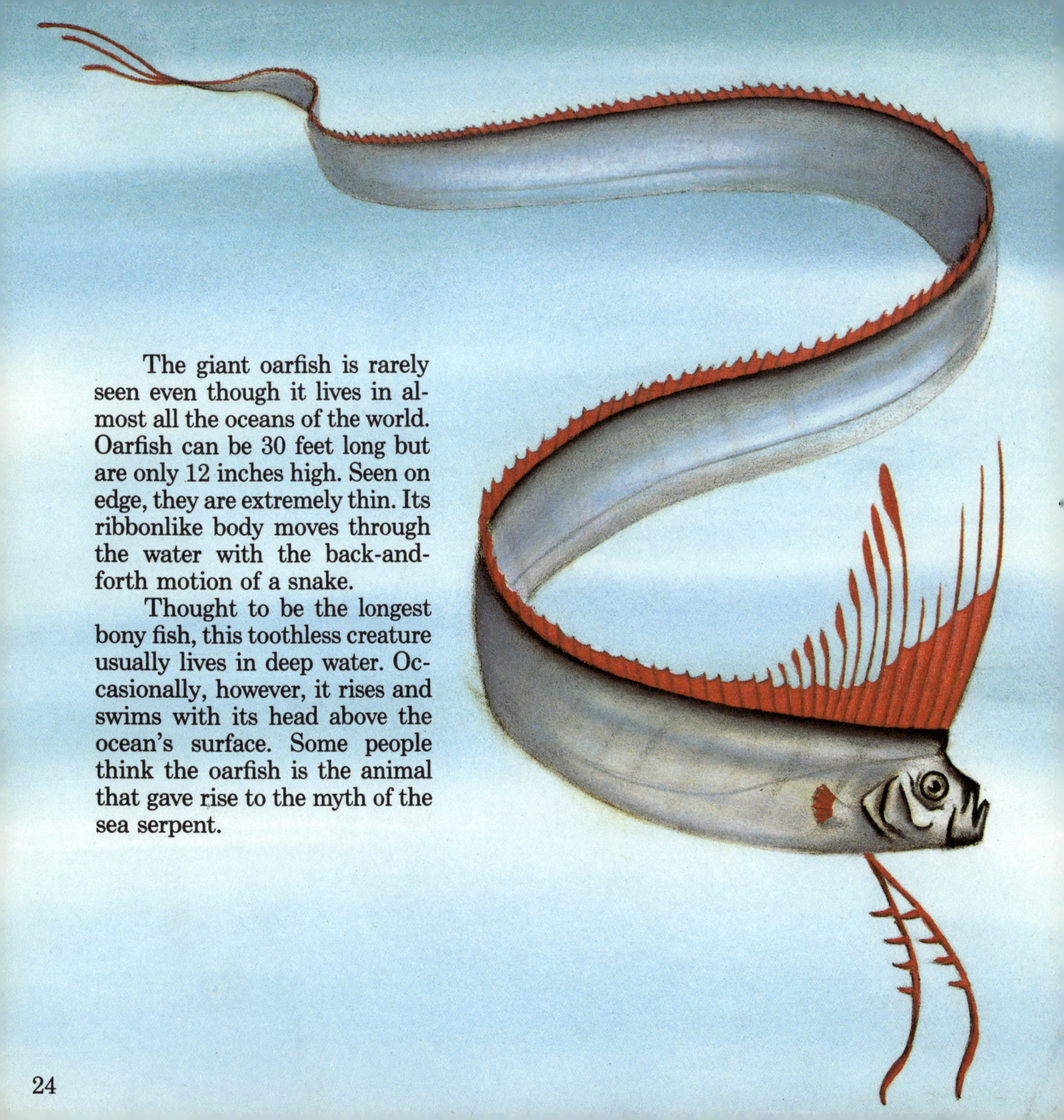

The giant oarfish is rarely seen even though it lives in almost all the oceans of the world. Oarfish can be 30 feet long but are only 12 inches high. Seen on edge, they are extremely thin. Its ribbonlike body moves through the water with the back-and-forth motion of a snake.

Thought to be the longest bony fish, this toothless creature usually lives in deep water. Occasionally, however, it rises and swims with its head above the ocean's surface. Some people think the oarfish is the animal that gave rise to the myth of the sea serpent.